# TRUMP

## SIGNS OF PROTEST

# TRUMP

## SIGNS OF PROTEST

**SCOTT EATON**

PORTICO

First published in the United Kingdom in 2019 by
Portico
43 Great Ormond Street
London
WC1N 3HZ

An imprint of Pavilion Books Company Ltd

ISBN 978-1-91162-238-3

A CIP catalogue record for this book is available from the British Library.

10 9 8 7 6 5 4 3 2 1

Reproduction by Rival Colour Ltd, UK
Printed and bound by L.E.G.O SpA
This book can be ordered direct from the publisher at www.pavilionbooks.com

# World vs Trump

We sit at a singular point in history. An accidental politician has stumbled onto the world stage who is so divisive and polarising in character and deed that he mobilises huge swathes of the world's population against him. I am, of course, referring to Donald Trump. This book documents the resistance of hundreds of thousands of people – of all ages, races, genders and nationalities – who have been moved to exercise their freedom of speech to oppose him in the most biting and satirical way. The outrage, disgust, and vitriol directed against Trump is pandemic … but so is the creativity and humour.

This book is clearly about protest, but on a grander scale is a testament to the fury of the masses who have singularly focused their outrage against Trump and his policies. Taken individually their work is raw, angry, explicit and mocking. But viewed collectively, it is a work of art … and creative genius.

While photographing the work in this book, I was in awe of the time, effort, and resources that people invested into crafting their pièces de résistance. I take no credit for the works presented here – I have only acted as the lens. This book, though, is a testament to the power and passion of the individuals who make up the global resistance to Donald Trump.

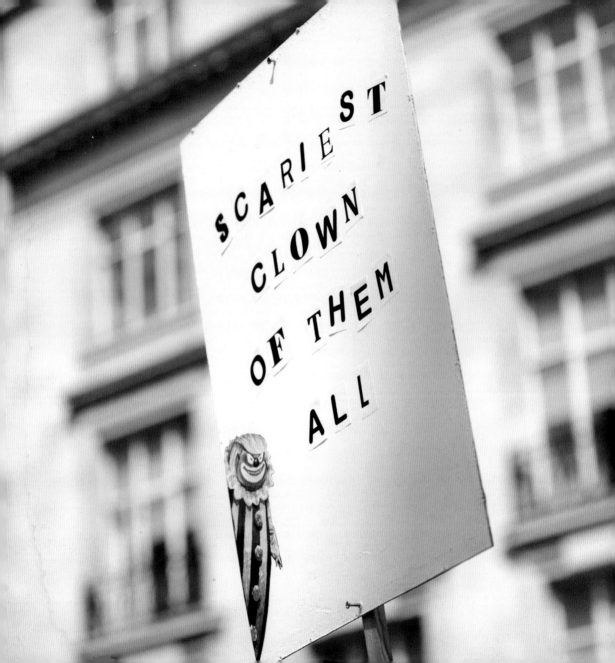

THE 45th PRESIDENT ?

TRUMP - PUTIN'S USEFUL IDIOT

America You can do better than this

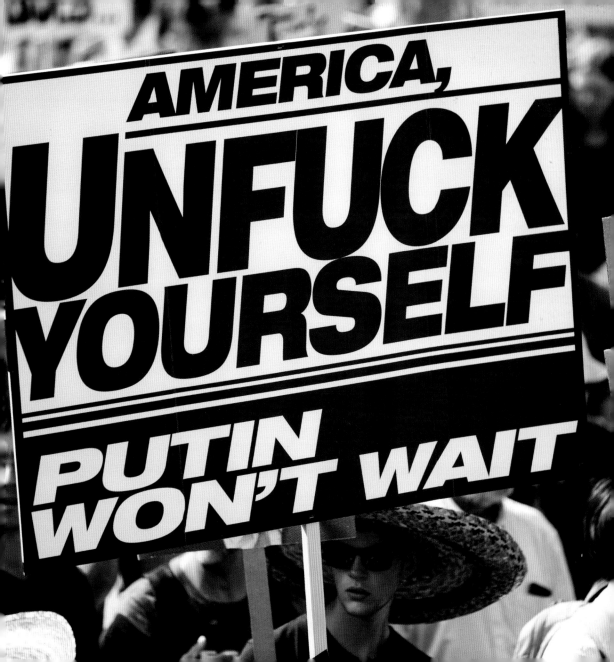

MAKING A~
~ HATE AGAIN

IL DUFUS

#D~
TR~

KICK
FASCIST
OUT THE
WHITE
HOUSE

FUCK OFF  FUCK ~
~ OFF  FUCK ~

"NOT THEN, NOT NOW"

MY

↘ ↙

Pussy

Grabs

BACK

FOA    FOA

An Angry
Pussy....
is
a GRABBED
Pussy !!!

Marching For
the 22 Women Who
accused you (There will be
hundreds More)
OF Sexual assault

Pussies bite →

ABUSERS NOT WELCOME

Politik-Ink.com

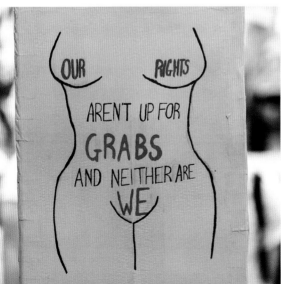

OUR RIGHTS ARENT UP FOR GRABS AND NEITHER ARE WE

WE NEED HOPE AND HUMANITY HUGS

ORANGE HUG

NOT UP FOR GRABS, DONALD!

BOTH: CORRUPT, VAIN, DELUSIONAL, AND HELD IN POWER BY THE KGB.

TRUMP IS AMERICA'S BREZHNEV

WAKE UP AMERICA!

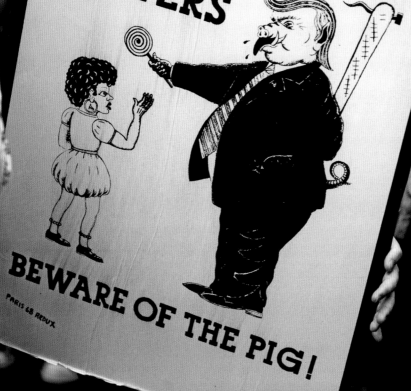

One nation DIVIDED,
Controlled by RELIGION,
with Liberty and Justice for
CIS WHITE MEN,
Land of the WHITE SUPREMACIST
Home of the BONE SPURS.

# Trump

\noun\

1. American bonehead
2. **Pull a Trump-**
to succeed despite idiocy
3. To expel intestinal gas
through the anus \slang\

Donald J. Trump

CHEETO-FACED, FERRET WEARING
SHITGIBBON

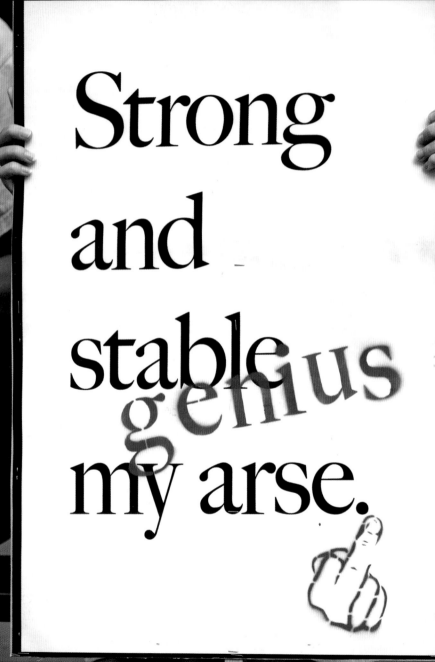

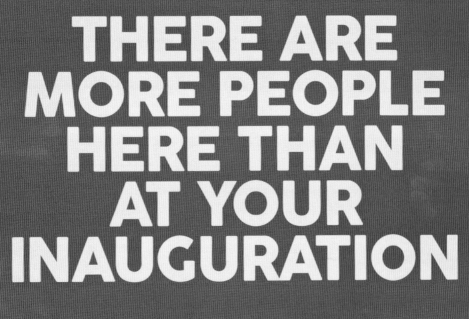

EARTH RAPIST*

*(ALSO WORKS IF YOU REMOVE THE WORD EARTH)

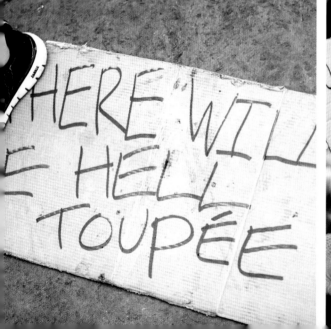

HERE WILL
E HELL
TOUPÉE

HOME

SCIENCE IS NOT
FAKE NEWS

MATE JUST
NOW

WE SHALL OVER
COMB

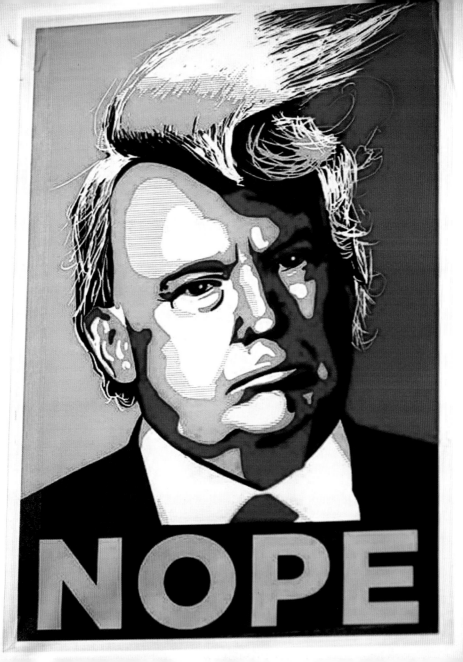

Tinkle, Tinkle, Little Czar

Putin Put you Where You Are!

Sad.

GO HOM

WE N

L♥VE AMERICA FUCK TRUMP

CA AG

TRUMP-GO TO PUTIN! THERE YOU ARE WELCOME

#DUMP TRUMP
ANTI-PALESTINE POLICIES ISLAMOPHOBIA & RACISM

LIAR LIAR PANTS ON FIRE

USA YOU ARE BETTER THAN THIS

bawbag
{scots}{noun} bawbag

{Trump} An utter fucking twat making a cunt of themselves and their country in public.

#DUMP TRUMP

#DUMP TRUMP

RESI

Fake?

Real.

Climate Action Now!

www.campaigncc.org

TRUMP

HOMOPHOBE
MISOGYNIST
RACIST
SEXIST
BIGOT
KNOB
ORANGE
COCK WOBBLE
DUMB
FUCKWIT
PRICK
PIG
GIT

NOT WELCOME

PILE OF VILE BILE

It's Sure One Helluva Stink Faks!

TRUMP
DUMP!
Shit
FAECES
CRAP
MERDE
拉屎
EXCREMENT
TURD
القرف
נ'הוד

There are not good people on both sides

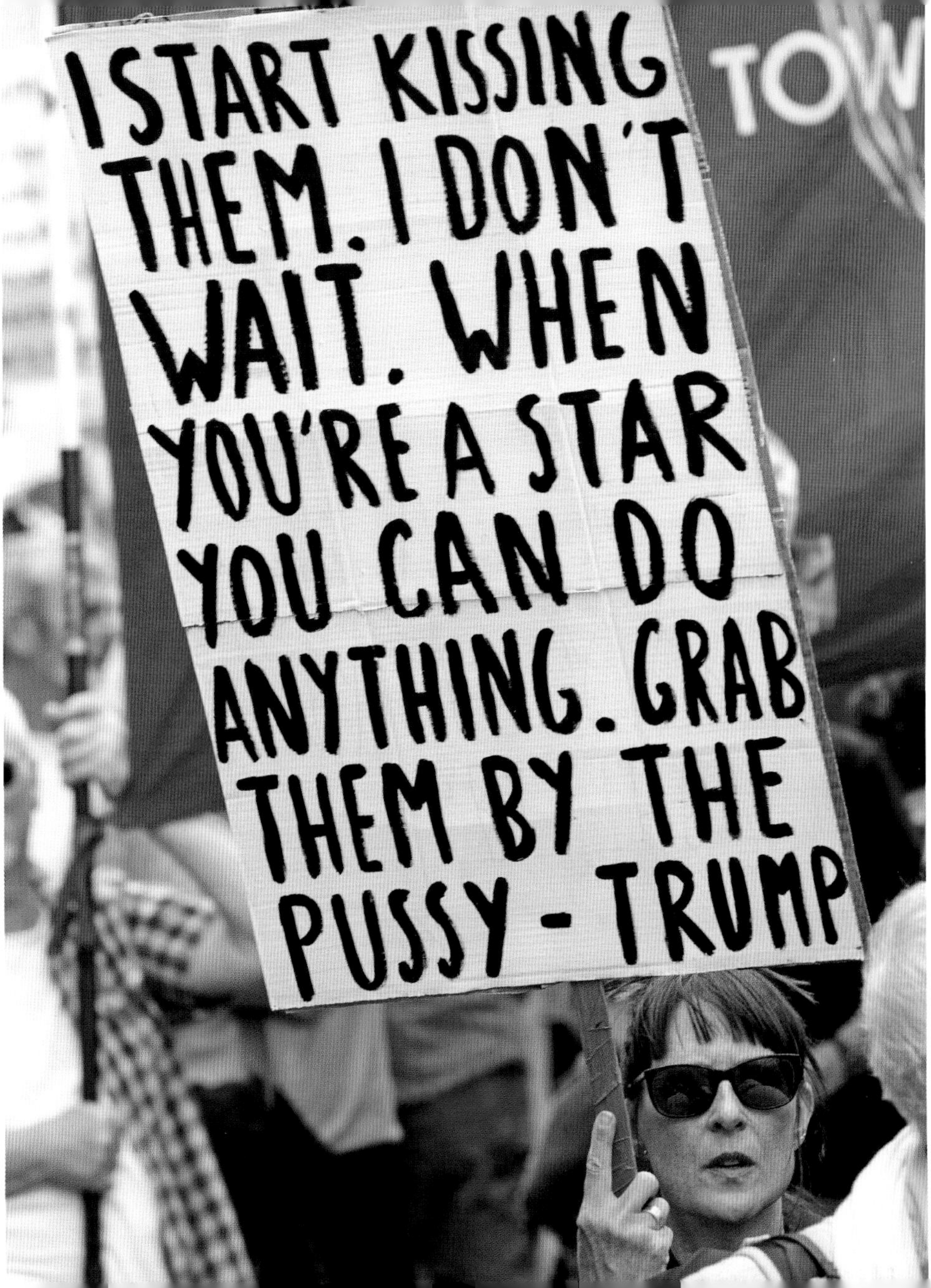
I START KISSING THEM. I DON'T WAIT. WHEN YOU'RE A STAR YOU CAN DO ANYTHING. GRAB THEM BY THE PUSSY - TRUMP
TOW

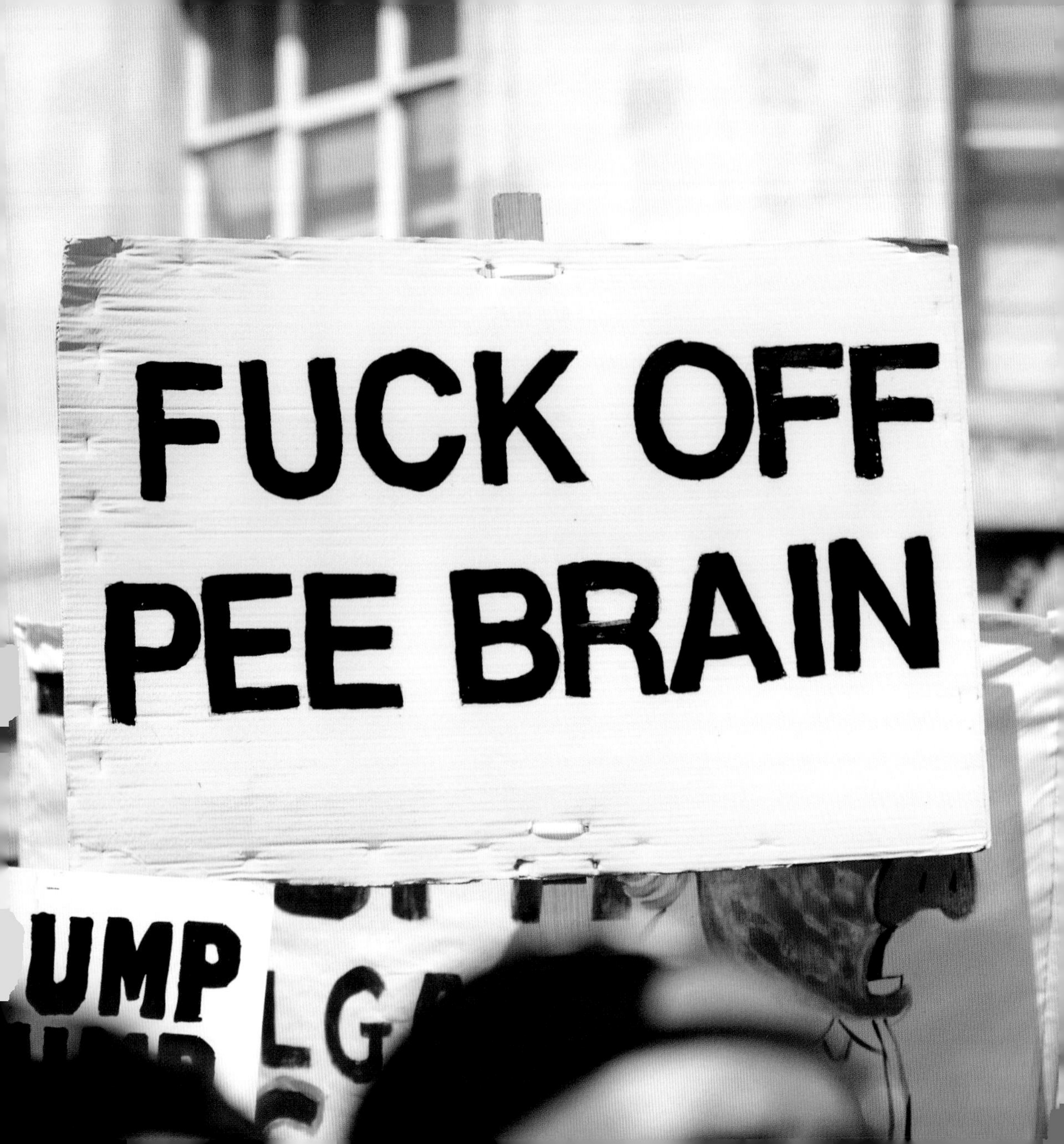
FUCK OFF
PEE BRAIN

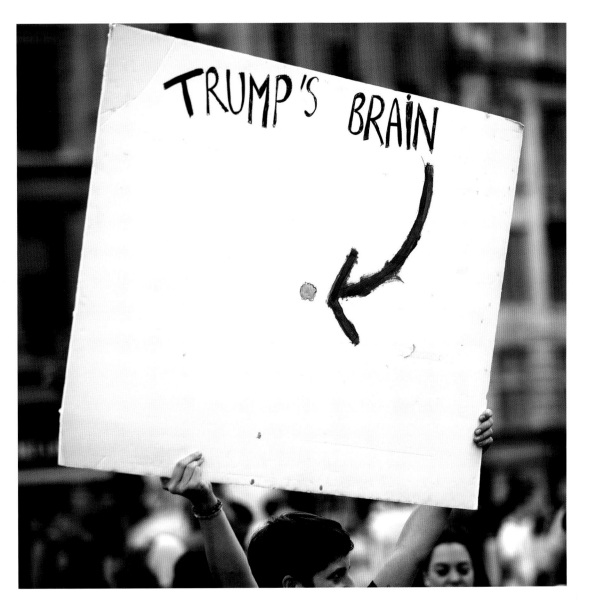

TANGERINE
TYRANT

PLEASE GO HOME!

STOP TRUMP

COME ON MUELLER
GRAB HIM BY THE CHEESY WOTSITS

WOTSIT RACIST

MAKE AMERICA A COLONY AGAIN

SAY NO TO THE FURIOUS ORANGE

THIN SKINNED

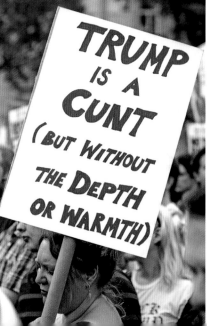

TRUMP IS A CUNT (BUT WITHOUT THE DEPTH OR WARMTH)

PUTTING THE "MOCK" INTO DEMOCRACY

SO CALLED
PRESIDENT TRUMP.
PERSONALITY DISORDERED
NARCISSIST.
PATHOLOGICAL LIAR.
MORALLY BANKRUPT.
A SEXIST, RACIST,
HOMOPHOBIC, XENOPHOBIC
BULLY.
UNFIT FOR OFFICE!

**TWO FACED RACIST USELESS MISOGYNISTIC PHONY**

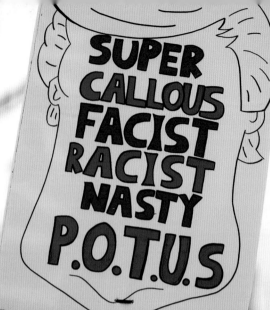

**SUPER CALLOUS FACIST RACIST NASTY P.O.T.U.S**

Pussy grabbing
Baby caging
Family breaking
Muslim hating
Klan lovin
Planet destroying
Racist spouting
Narcissistic bragging
Dictator adoring
Lacking all
Decency

LIAR
THUG
SURPER
MISOGYNIST
PUTIN'S PUPPET

#DUMP TRUMP

BANK

**D.T.**

THE EXTRA-TERRESTRIAL
IN HIS ADVENTURE ON EARTH

DONT LIKE TRUMP HIS
RESIDENCY IS A FLUM
UT MOST OF ALL HE?
A BIG ORANGE
CUNT

ANTI-PALESTINE
#DUMPTRUMP
FOA

S.AMOPHOBI
#DUMPTRUMP
FOA

#DUMP
TRUMP

DONALD TRUMP IS A COCK WOBBLE

TRUMP tiny hands MASSIVE TWAT

DOWN WITH THIS SORT OF THING

TINY HANDS, TREMENDOUS ASSHOLE

# AT LEAST HITLER DID SOME PAINTING

PATHOLOGICAL LIAR
MORALLY BANKRUPT.
A SEXIST, RACIST,
HOMOPHOBIC, XENOPHOBIC
BULLY
UNFIT FOR OFFICE!

MP
NOT
WELCOME

RESIST
RESIST
RESIST
RESIST
RESIST

No to
Trump
NOT

DO ALL

TRUMP
NOT
WELCOME
TOGETHER AGAINST TRUMP

NO TO
RACISM

NO TO
RACISM

SAY NO
TO TRUMP
WORLD'S
#1 RACIST

TRUMP
NOT
WELCOME

NO
RA

NO
RA

FIGHT TRUMPISM

FIGHT
SEXISM

TO A
CAU

BRE

#DUMP
TRUMP

DUMP
MP

#DUMP
TRUMP

FIGHT TRUMPISM
FIGHT
IALISM
ght for
ialism.

STAND UP
RACISM

SAY
TO

DECENT     FOLK     OPPOSE     HATE

Pussy grabbing
Baby caging
Family breaking
Muslim hating
Klan lovin
Planet destroying
Racist spouting
Narcissistic bragging
Dictator adoring
Lacking all
Decency

NO TO HATE

BUILD THAT WALL

One Earth
You've been Trumped

Pussy grabbing
Baby caging
Family breaking
Muslim hating
Klan lovin
Planet destroying
Racist spouting
Narcissistic bragging
Dictator adoring
Lacking all
Decency

NOT WELCOME

BIGLY

PISS OFF CIRCUS

Stand against the right.

CAGE THE BABY

THE ONLY BABY WHO

NO-ONE PUTS BABY IN THE CORNER!

SHOULD BE IN A CAGE

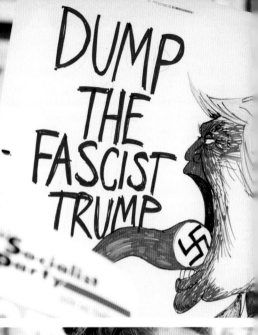

TRUMP

SAFETY MATCHES
· redneck-friendly
· ignites sons of bitches

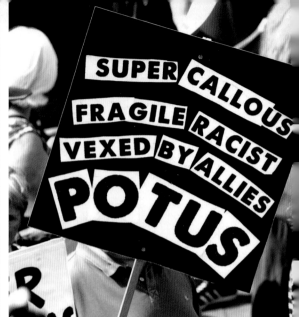

SUPER CALLOUS
FRAGILE RACIST
VEXED BY ALLIES
POTUS

WE LOVE
immigrants

#DUM
RUMI

THEY MAKE GREAT
SCAPEGOATS

THERE COMES
TIME WHEN...
SILENCE
IS BETRAYAL
THAT TIME IS
NOW PAST

RESIS

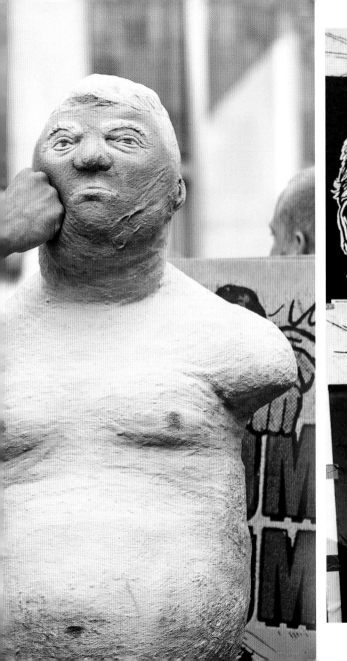

EVERYONE HATES YOU
DONALD

Super CALLOUS
FASCIST RACIST
SEXIST 'LOSER'
POTUS
GET YOUR TINY HANDS
OFF MY RIGHTS
AND S
AY
IS REALLY QUITE ATROCIOUS

I came off
FORTNITE
for this!

UNCIVIL AMERICANS
AGAINST UNELECTED TRUMP

FUCK PUTIN ELECTION HACKING
TO HELL WITH USEFUL IDIOTS
GET SCREWED, ACCELERATIONIST
SUCK IT, FASCISTS
DAMN THE APOLOGIST

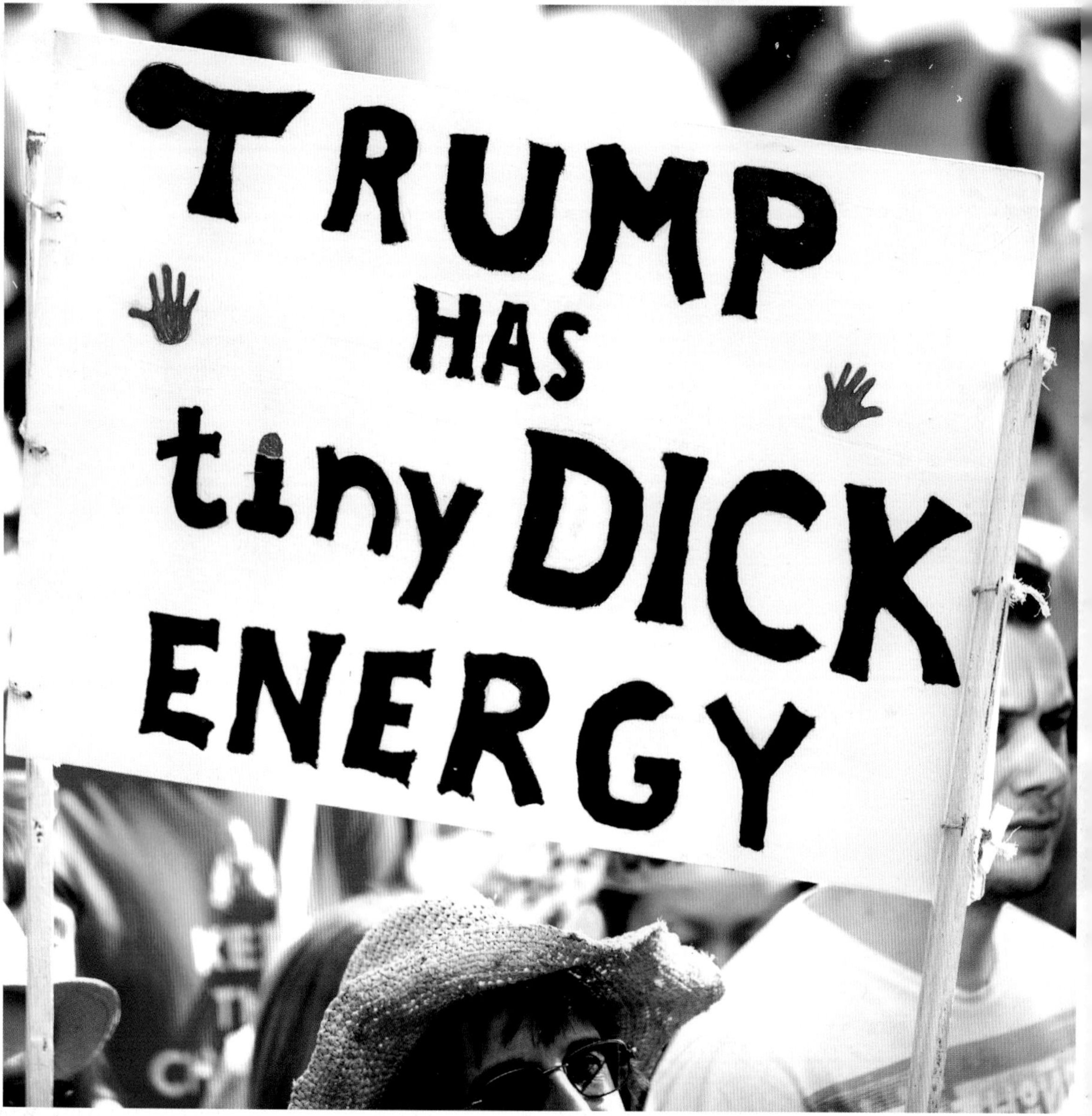
TRUMP
HAS
tiny DICK
ENERGY

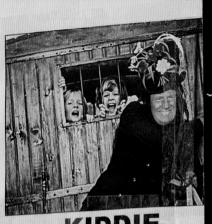

KIDDIE
KATCHING
KUNT

CAGED
BY
TRUMP

FASCIST
CHILD
SNATCHERS
AREN'T
WELCOME
HERE

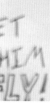

NO

PUTS BA

IN A COR

ET
HIM
LY!

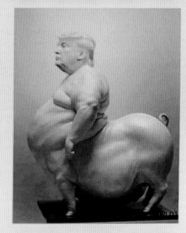

**PIGOT**

**UNWANTED**

**DEAD OR ALIVE**

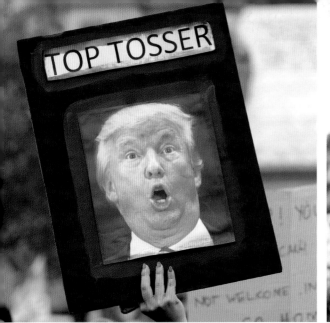

ANOTHER PATRIOTIC AMERICAN

WHODESPISES TRUMP

I NEVER THOUGHT I'D MISS NIXON

THE U.S. is a NATION of IMMIGRANTS you AMERICAN IDIOT

♥ USA / TRUMP

THE CHILD CATCHER-IN-CHIEF
STAND UP TO EVIL!

#BASTA # FAMILIES BELONG TOGETHER

REFUGEES IN
FASCISTS OUT

WHAT
THE
FUCK
YOU!

Humanity
Against
Trump

LOCK U
THE
P****
GRABBER!

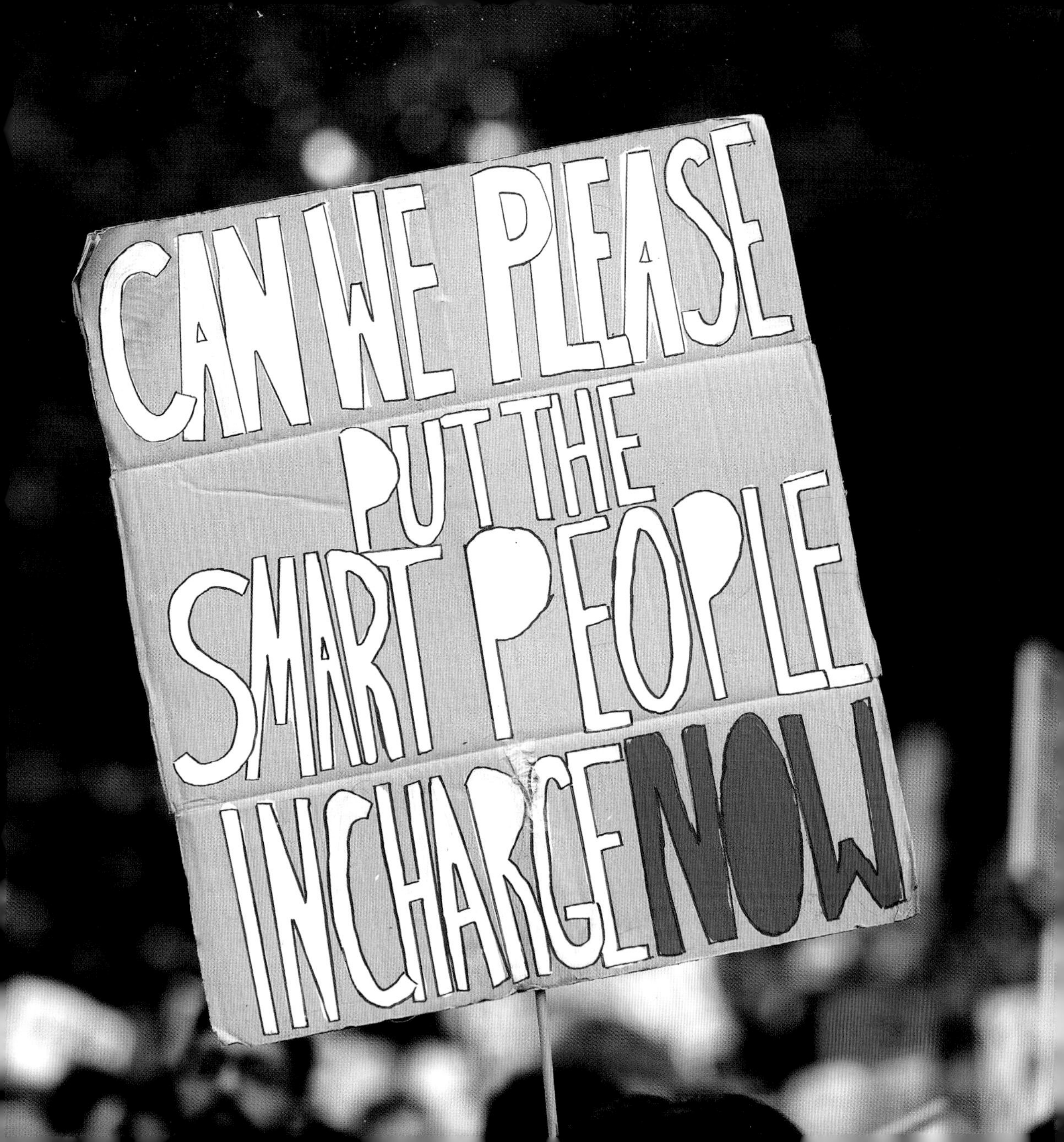
CAN WE PLEASE
PUT THE
SMART PEOPLE
IN CHARGE NOW

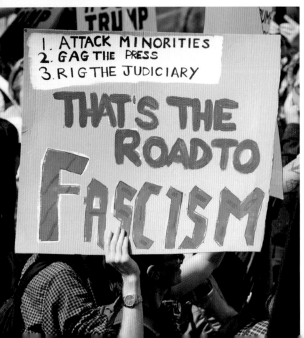

FASCISM IS ON THE RISE

# PANIC

### AND

# TAKE

# ACTION

COMPLACENCY IS COMPLICITY